LACROSSE

LACROSSE

How to Play and Win

Arnold Madison

David McKay Company, Inc.
New York

Library of Congress Cataloging in Publication Data

Madison, Arnold.
Lacrosse : how to play and win.

1. Lacrosse. I. Title.
GV999.M26   796.34'7   78-4533
ISBN 0-679-20775-9

1 2 3 4 5 6 7 8 9 10

MANUFACTURED IN THE UNITED STATES OF AMERICA

ILLUSTRATION CREDITS

Black Star, page 26; The Canadian Lacrosse Hall of Fame, page 15; Choate Rosemary Hall, Wallingford, Connecticut, page 54; The Emma Willard School, Troy, New York, page 56 bottom; Free Lance Photographers Guild, Inc., page 12; Free Lance Photographers Guild, Inc., Photographer: Michael L. Valeri, page 2 left; Photographs from *Lacrosse* by Bob Scott. Copyrighted 1976 by The Johns Hopkins University Press. Photographer: Bob Rothgaber, pages 18, 36, 37, 39, 40, 42, 47-49; The Lacrosse Foundation, Inc., Lacrosse Hall of Fame Museum, pages 11, 13, 57; The Lacrosse Foundation, Inc., Lacrosse Hall of Fame Museum, U.S. Army photograph, page 14; Line drawings on page 4 by Nils Ostberg; Public Archives Canada C-8695, page 8, C-22982, page 10; The Taft School, Watertown, Connecticut, page 2 bottom, 28, 58 Photographer: Brad Joblin; Wilton Lacrosse Association, title page, page 29, 56 top; Diagram on page 55 by Pat Maclea, courtesy of the Wilton Lacrosse Association.

Contents

Thud! Crack! Swish!

A low murmur ripples through the waiting crowd. The fourth quarter will begin in a few moments. The score is close—too close. Nine-eight. New York has that slim one-point lead over Maryland.

The day is a warm Saturday. Lacrosse is a spring game, and everyone enjoys sitting outdoors on this mild afternoon. But no one is relaxed. The game so far has been a fast-paced, teeth-jarring match. The two teams are evenly matched.

The players trot onto the field and take their places. Maryland wears bright red uniforms; New York wears black and gold. The two centers line their sticks on the middle X. They crouch like tight springs about to uncoil. The small white ball rests between the netted pockets of their sticks.

A whistle bleeps, and the crowd roars.

The centers battle for the ball. Sticks clack as Maryland player 25 does a quick stick check. But he is unsuccessful because New York midfielder 72 has the ball. He does a quick roll dodge around his defender and is off toward the goal.

Evidence of the popularity of lacrosse in the United States is the growth of professional box lacrosse teams, such as the Boston Bolts and New York Tomahawks.

The number of school and college lacrosse teams increases each year.

But other Maryland defense players move toward 72, smothering him in red. Bodies thud as checks are thrown. The white ball moves through the air like a daytime shooting star. From New York 16 to New York 53 and back to New York 72. A black and gold New York attack hovers behind the Maryland goal like a bumblebee waiting for the first scent of nectar.

Suddenly, he reaches up and snares the ball. He fakes a pass to the right and snaps the ball to New York 17 who is cutting toward the goal. Number 17 quick-wrists the ball into the goal before the goalie can swing completely around. The ball swishes against the goal net.

The score is ten-eight—with nine minutes to go.

There is no rest for the sweating players because the game continues. Lacrosse has been called the "fastest game on two feet." Today's match proves that fact. Lacrosse is also an exciting, fascinating game for both fan and player.

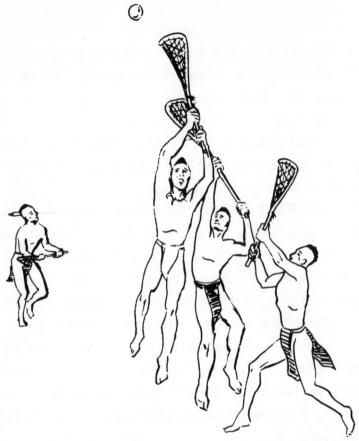

Lacrosse, or "little-brother-of-war," was the most popular ball game of the North American Indians—from Hudson Bay to the Gulf of Mexico, and from the Atlantic coast to the Plains.

This pair of Oto lacrosse sticks were made of hardwood, bent at the ends into semi-hoops crossed with rawhide thongs.

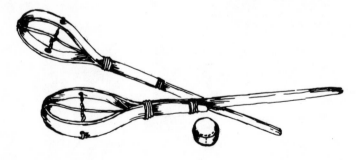

A Brief History

Few modern sports have had as colorful a history as lacrosse. The beginnings range back before the written history of Native Americans. When the first European explorers arrived in North America, they found some form of lacrosse being played by the Sioux, Cherokee, Chippewa, Mohawk, and many other tribes. Few early names for the game have survived, but the Ojibwa name is probably the best remembered: *baggattaway*.

French settlers gave the sport the name which is used today. They noticed that the sticks used by Native American players were similar to the *crosier (la crosse)* carried by bishops as a symbol of their office. The bishop's *crosier* was like a shepherd's crook in size and length. The Indian sticks were three to four feet long, with a netted hoop at one end. In some areas, two smaller sticks were used—one in each hand.

In 1636, a Jesuit missionary, Jean de Brébeuf, was the first to title the game *crosse* after he had watched the Hurons in a contest. Over the years, the name has changed into the single word, lacrosse.

The original sport was different in other ways than

the modern game. For example, there were no set numbers for the teams. Team size could vary from a few players to over a thousand men. Only Indian males were allowed to engage in the event. The women and children watched from the sidelines. But the audiences were enthusiastic. If a player did not perform at top capacity, the women would surge onto the field and beat him with switches. This could be painful. Early players did not wear the heavily padded suits seen today. They wore only breechcloths and usually played barefooted.

If the players had to watch out for unhappy fans, the crowd had to keep an eye on the swiftly moving teams. No official sidelines were set for the game. Players could charge in any direction. Frequently, onlookers had to scramble for safety as hundreds of sweating players pounded toward them.

The goals might be a tree, rock, or two posts six to nine feet apart. If a single pole was used, the object of the game was to hit the goal with the ball, which was about the size of a tennis ball. It was usually made of wood or deerskin padded with moss or deer hair. The distance between the two teams' goals depended upon the locale. As a rule, the goals were set about 500 yards to a half mile away from each other. But some games had goals several miles apart.

Not only was there freedom in field length, but no tight limits were placed on game time. The contests sometimes lasted two to three days, starting each day at sunup and ending at sundown. Clearly, the players needed great physical strength. For that reason, tribes often trained their braves by having them engage in lacrosse games. The roughness of the sport conditioned the men for close combat and developed endurance for hunting and warring parties.

Lacrosse was not only played for fun or for training would-be warriors. Tribes used the sport for military tactics, also. On June 4, 1763, an historic game was played outside a British fort in Canada. The Ojibwas and Sacks staged a match supposedly to honor the birthday of King George III. People in the garrison came out to watch the game. As the players dashed through the crowd, tribespeople handed them hidden weapons. The braves then invaded the fort. They destroyed the buildings and killed most of the soldiers and civilians.

After the Revolutionary War, lacrosse gradually became more organized. Teams were composed of sixty men, and the playing field was set at about 500 yards. By 1825, team size had shrunk to seven players who performed on a fifty-yard field. Great tribal honor awaited any brave chosen for these teams.

The French and British settlers began taking an active part in the game. The long years of lacrosse training, however, continued to make the Native Americans better players than the white men. In 1844, a team of five Native Americans easily defeated seven white people. Seven years would pass before a white team could claim victory.

Interest in lacrosse was spreading. The Montreal

William George Beers, a Canadian dentist-poet-song writer, was the "Father of Lacrosse." He was the first to set down official rules for the game. Beers also introduced the India-rubber sponge ball that replaced the Indian hair-stuffed ball.

Lacrosse Club was formed in 1856. The white man's entry also introduced changes which improved the game. A longer stick was made with a wide, triangular netting which was tightly strung. The improved stick gave birth to new techniques. Passing and teamwork were now seen on the field.

In 1867, lacrosse was named the national sport of

Canada. This happened on the same day the Dominion of Canada was created. At the beginning of that year, only six clubs played in Canada. By the end of the year, eighty clubs competed in the sport.

Like other sports, lacrosse has its 'father.' Dr. W. George Beers became known as the 'father of lacrosse.' He organized the game and helped spread its popularity. Dr. Beers, a Montreal dentist, formed the Canadian National Lacrosse Association. He also drew up the first set of written rules.

A time limit was now set. Other changes were molding the game into today's form. The goal posts were placed seven feet apart. A ribbon stretched across the top of the poles. This would change into the modern goal net.

Lacrosse fever was, indeed, catching. The game moved from Canada to England and finally to the United States. In 1867, a lacrosse demonstration was presented at the Saratoga Springs, New York, fairground. A year later, the first lacrosse club was organized in the United States: the Mohawk Club of Troy, New York. In that year, the Mohawk Club played and lost four games to Canadian clubs. But U.S. residents welcomed the new sport.

Lacrosse was called the "most exciting and at the same time the most laughter provoking among the whole range of outdoor sports," by the New York *World* in 1868.

By 1879, lacrosse had moved south and west. But interest centered around New York, Boston, Phila-

Even in 1919, each quarter began with a face-off. Canadian teams from Victoria and Winnipeg battled for the prized Mann Cup. Final score: Victoria 17, Winnipeg 7.

delphia, and Baltimore. Colleges seized the new game and formed teams. Harvard was named the first Inter-collegiate Champion 1881. The service academies joined the competition in the early nineteen hundreds: Army, 1907; Navy, 1908.

The 1900s saw more changes. In 1921, the offside rule was made official. The field was divided by a center line, and each team had to keep at least three players in

Lee Chambers was a star Navy attackperson in the late 1940s.

In the 1950s, sixteen American lacrosse players toured England. One stop was at the famous girls' public school at Roedean, where the visitors took part in a "Lacrosse Holiday."

each half of the field. This did not include the goal-keepers. The modern square goal replaced the early poles. And, in the 1930s, the helmet and mask that are now required gear came into use.

Like ever-widening circles in a pool, lacrosse spread around the world—New Zealand, Australia, and, at times, the International Olympic Games. In addition, high schools formed lacrosse teams. In 1951, thirty-eight high

Don O'Neill, a member of the Dickinson College Lacrosse
team, was the nation's top amateur scorer in 1958.

Cadet Norm Webb was an All-American team member of Army's 1964 squad.

schools had lacrosse teams. Today, over 400 high school teams compete against each other.

Little League lacrosse was born in Baltimore, Maryland in 1959. What started as three teams has now grown to over fifty teams.

The game, which has progressed from a wild free-for-all, has become a well-regulated sport. Let us take a look at modern lacrosse.

The Field, Players, and Equipment

There are two types of lacrosse: field and box. Box lacrosse is very popular in Canada. Games are played on indoor ice hockey arenas. There are six players on a box lacrosse team as compared to ten players on a field squad. The game has much action and physical contact. Therefore, the sport resembles ice hockey more than field lacrosse. The latter is also played in Canada, but this type

Box lacrosse is tremendously popular in Canada. The fast-paced game is played on indoor courts and features much physical contact.

of lacrosse is the major form of the game in the United States.

The Field

The size of the playing field varies. The length is a standard 110 yards, but the width may range from 53⅓ to 60 yards. Sixty yards is considered the official width of a field. The reason for the shifting measurements is the scarcity of fields built solely for lacrosse. Many school and community clubs have to use a football field. Football fields have a width of 53⅓ yards.

The goals are centered on the field eighty yards apart. This permits an area of fifteen yards behind each goal. Thus, lacrosse has even greater possibilities to work from the rear of the goal than does ice hockey. A circle, 18 feet in diameter, is marked around each goal. This circle is called the *crease*.

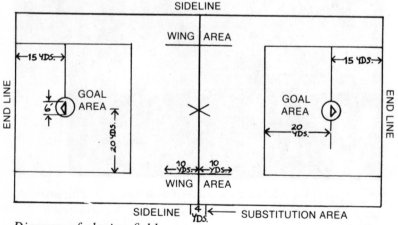

Diagram of playing field.

The goal itself is constructed of two vertical posts, joined by a top crossbar six feet above the ground. The posts are six feet apart. A ground line is drawn across the front of the goal opening, connecting the two upright posts. This marker is the *goal line.* A pyramid-shaped net backs the goal and is connected to the ground seven feet behind the goal. In order to score one point, a player must move the ball through the opening formed by the three bars and the goal line.

A 35 by 40-yard rectangle is drawn around each goal. These lines show the *goal area.* The length of the field is divided by a center line. An X is placed in the middle of the line and is known as the *center of the field.*

One more area is found on the sidelines of a lacrosse field: the *substitution area.* This is a four-yard wide space, marked two yards each direction from the center line. The substitute section is next to the timer's table.

The Players

A lacrosse team consists of ten players and any number of substitutes. These players handle the four basic positions: goal, defense, midfield, and attack.

The *goalkeeper,* or goalie, is stationed directly in front of the goal line. If an opposing player manages to escape the rest of the team, the goalie tries to prevent a point from being scored.

Many people call the goalkeeper the most courageous person on a team. This individual must not be

A goalkeeper about to prevent an opponent from scoring.

afraid to be struck by a solid rubber ball traveling up to ninety miles an hour. Between forty and sixty shots may be fired at the goalie during a game. They often come from a distance less than twenty-five feet away.

Leadership qualities are highly desirable because the goalie directs the position of each person on the defensive half of the field. Size is not important. A coach most often seeks a goalkeeper who is extra quick to stop a ball.

Because the goalie is the last line of defense for a

team, blame may be placed on him or her if a point is scored. The goalkeeper should be willing to take criticism even if there has been no way to prevent that point. Goalkeepers, should not be people who blame others for their mistakes or poor judgment.

The goalie is supported by three *defensepersons.* Because these players usually perform on the crease, they are also known as the "crease defensepersons" or "close defense." The three players generally stay near the goal. Therefore, they fulfill the offside rule which is special to the game of lacrosse. This rule states that a team must have four players on the defensive half of the field at all times. Defensepersons do not become as tired as other players because they remain on one half of the field. So these players will usually play during an entire game.

Defensepersons have much pressure placed on them during a game. Their job is to prevent an opponent from taking a close shot at the goal. The defense stays with the other team's attackperson. Size can be helpful in playing this position. A defenseperson might want to reach over the opposing player. Quick reactions and stick work are extremely important. Patience, however, is also needed. A person who becomes overly anxious could commit a foul or lose a dodging opponent.

Three *midfielders* play the entire field. They handle either offensive or defensive playing, depending upon the position of the ball. One player is called the "center." Midfielders may run full speed up and down the field as many as five times without stopping. In between those sprints, they may have to battle for a loose ball. Therefore, a midfielder is given rest periods while a substitute takes over the position.

Midfielders need to have great stamina and endurance. They are the scramblers of the lacrosse team. Two other qualities are also needed: fast stick work and shooting ability. Often coaches select one midfielder who is especially good at handling the stick, but only an average shot. Another midfielder would be chosen for shooting ability, although the person might be slower with a stick. Playing defense is one of the most important jobs of the midfielder so the player should have quick reactions and movements.

There are three more positions on a lacrosse team. The *attackpersons* are usually found around the opponent's goal. Thus, they fulfill the requirement of the second half of the offside rule. Each team must have three players on the opponent's half of the field at all times. The attackpersons are also known as the "close attacks."

One attack plays on the opponent's crease and is called the *crease attackperson.* The other two attacks generally stay behind the goal, running around the front of the cage to shoot. At other times they pass the ball to teammates and act as the squad's *feeders.*

All three attacks should be able to handle the stick right- or left-handed. The crease attack should be the best shot on the team. The two players who stay behind the goal should be excellent dodgers and feeders.

The attack needs to be tough enough to absorb the body checks of the opponent's defense. Attackpersons must also be mentally alert. They have to direct the offensive play as well as decide when to shoot or pass.

People who wish to play lacrosse have to be able to view themselves objectively. If an athlete is below average but has speed, the person could play midfield or defense. Lacking speed, however, would mean the defense position would be the best choice. An average athlete with speed could handle any slot. This individual might well become an excellent defenseperson or midfielder. The above-average athlete, also, could play any position. The coach will probably use that person as an attack due to the player's scoring ability.

No matter what role a player selects, he or she will find the game of lacrosse exciting and challenging.

The Ball and the Sticks

Lacrosse is played with a small, hard rubber ball weighing about five ounces. The ball is white or orange and is slightly smaller than a baseball, but just as hard. A rule states that the ball must have a certain bounce power. The test is to drop the ball from a height of six feet onto a hard wooden floor. The ball must bounce forty-three to fifty-one inches.

During a game, the players propel the ball in any direction. They are not permitted to touch the ball with their hands, but they are allowed to kick the ball. However, most of the time they bat the ball with the stick.

The lacrosse stick was originally called the *crosse*—a name that is dying out. There are four different kinds of stick. No matter which kind is used, the stick will have the same basic parts.

The *head* of the stick is roughly triangular, and contains the netted pocket. The net may be made of cord, nylon, linen, or any synthetic material. The tension of the netting can be adjusted. A ball is placed in the pocket. If the upper edge of the ball is not even with the top of the pocket, the net is too loose.

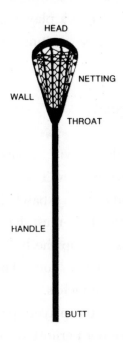

HEAD

NETTING

WALL

THROAT

HANDLE

BUTT

The *handle*, or body of the stick, was at one time hand-made. Since the early 1970s, a machine-made plastic stick, with either a wooden or aluminum handle, has been widely used. The tip of the handle is called the *butt*.

The overall length of the stick is between forty and seventy-two inches, depending upon the player's position. An attack uses the shortest stick, while the defense usually has the longest. The inside measurement of the head also varies. A goalkeeper generally prefers a twelve-inch head, while most midfielders and attackpersons use a 6½- or 7-inch head. The defense player, especially the close defense, prefers an eight-inch head.

Personal Equipment

Many schools and lacrosse clubs find they can adapt other sports equipment if funds are not available to buy special gear. Regulations require lacrosse players to wear helmets equipped with face masks. A lacrosse helmet is lighter than a football helmet; a cupped chin strap holds it in place. Football requires much more physical contact than lacrosse. Football helmets, however, can be fitted with a face mask and used for lacrosse.

A player must also wear gloves. Many lacrosse players use ice hockey gloves. But a glove with a moveable thumb is better. Lacrosse gloves are made with or without palms. Many players cut out the palm and the inside portion of the glove fingers. This gives them better control of the stick with their hands.

Although arm pads and shoulder pads are not required, most coaches insist that their players wear them for extra safety.

Other personal equipment includes a jersey top, shorts, and shoes. A football jersey can be worn as can soccer or basketball shorts. Cleated football or soccer shoes are excellent for lacrosse.

Now that the basic field and playing positions have been explained, let's check the general rules of the game.

Playing the Game

Junior and high school lacrosse is played in four periods of ten minutes each. College lacrosse is a longer game, consisting of four periods of fifteen minutes each. Should overtime be needed, schools play two periods, each three minutes long. Colleges have two periods, also, but each lasts four minutes. If the score is still tied, a sudden-death play is put into action. The team which scores the first point is the winner of the school or college event.

The game is under the control of two officials: an umpire and a referee. The referee has the final word in any decision. These officials begin each quarter and re-new the game after a goal with a *face-off*.

During the opening face-off, the two centers are in the center of the field. The ball is placed on the X between their sticks. The players crouch, their feet about hip-width apart. The right hand grips the stick's throat, the left hand is placed further down, but no closer than eighteen inches to the right hand.

When the whistle blows, the centers battle for the ball. The midfielders help the center. The attack and defense players remain behind their lines. They are free to move about if a team gets possession of the ball or if the ball rolls over one of their lines. They are also freed if the ball goes out of bounds.

If a player throws or carries the ball out of bounds, the opposing team is given possession of the ball. This is

Two centers perform a face-off at the start of an opening game.

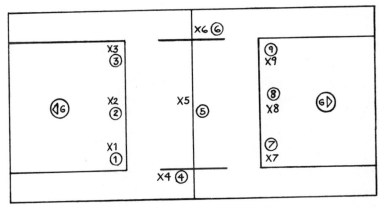

Diagram of field, with players indicated at the beginning of the game.

true of most sports. In lacrosse, however, there is an exception. This occurs if someone attempts a goal shot, misses, and the ball goes out of bounds. Possession is given to the team which had a player closest to the ball when it crossed the boundary.

The team that gained the ball during the face-off moves forward in its attack, passing the ball from one player to another. The opposing team falls into a defensive position. The goal must be guarded. Also, they must try to cause the other team to lose control of the ball.

Checks are permitted in the struggle. There are body checks and stick checks. Body checking is legal if the other player has the ball or is within five yards of a loose ball. Contact with the other person can only be made from the front and side and above the knees. A stick check can be made under the same conditions. The

Junior and high-school lacrosse is usually played in four periods of ten minutes each.

player's gloved hand gripping the stick is ruled as part of the stick. Therefore, that hand may be checked. No other part of the body may be checked with the stick, however. Wild swinging of the stick to stop an opponent is illegal.

Breaking these rules results in penalties against the team or player. Lacrosse is similar to ice hockey. A penalized player is placed in the penalty box. The team then operates with one less person. Penalties vary from thirty seconds to three minutes.

A five-person team cannot prevent a six-person team from getting at least one good shot at the goal in that minute of penalization. Therefore, players who continually break the rules are benched by the coach. Coaches cannot have five-person teams on a lacrosse field and hope for victory.

There are two types of fouls: technical and personal. The technical fouls are the less serious. They include:

- Interference with a player who does not have the ball or is not within five yards of the ball.
- Throwing the stick.
- Pushing an opponent with the body or a stick from the rear.
- Holding the opponent's stick or body.
- Lying on the ball or trapping the ball with the stick. (A player may trap a ball no longer than is needed to control it and pick up the ball in one continuous movement.)
- Offside. Failure to observe the offside rule.

If the offending team does not have the ball when a technical foul is committed, the player is suspended for thirty seconds. If the team does have the ball, the opposing team is given possession. This would also happen if neither team had possession of the ball when the foul occurred.

Personal fouls are more serious. The following would be considered personal fouls:

- Illegal body checking.
- Tripping—striking the opponent below the knees with the stick, arms, hands, feet or legs.
- Unsportsmanlike conduct, such as speaking in profane, threatening, or obscene language to an opposing player or official.
- Deliberately attempting to strike or striking an opponent or official with fist or stick.

Because personal fouls are viewed more seriously, the penalties are longer than for technical fouls. For most personal fouls, one minute is required in the penalty box. There are also expulsion fouls. These can be called against a person who tries to hit or strikes an opposing player or official. The player is assigned three minutes in the box and is not permitted to re-enter the game. The player's substitute may not take his or her place until the three minutes have passed.

For lesser penalties, there are ways for the player to leave the box before the full time has gone by. For example, the coach may substitute another player for the guilty one. If the opposing team scores a goal, the person is released. This happens, also, if the penalized team gets possession of the ball in its attack-goal area.

Lacrosse has a special foul rule which is similar to ice hockey. This involves a defending player who fouls an attacking player who has possession of the ball. The foul is committed in the attack half of the field. If this happens, the official uses the *slow-whistle* technique. The scoring play is allowed to continue, but the official drops a signal flag. A scoring play is completed when the attacking team loses control of the ball. Taking a shot or failing to move toward the goal also signals the end of a scoring play. Only one shot is permitted during a slow-whistle play.

Lacrosse has been described as a "wide open game with a good deal of body contact." This is true. Often, however, people who do not know lacrosse think the sport is rough. They see the game as one in which people "swing sticks at each other."

This is a totally false picture. Body contact may happen frequently, but lacrosse players suffer serious injuries less often than players of other sports. Lacrosse is a well-regulated game which requires intelligence, skill, and good physical conditioning.

Stick Work

Learning how to handle the lacrosse stick is perhaps the most important skill a player needs to develop. Even college varsity players practice catching, throwing, cradling, and scooping the ball.

If you purchase a lacrosse stick, there are steps to follow. A new stick needs to be broken in. This can be done within a few days. Don't try to break in the netting by pushing and pulling the material. This will create a pocket which may not fit your playing. The best way to break in a new stick is to simply play catch with it for a few days. By doing this, the pocket will be formed and it will fit your style.

At first, the pocket netting will be tight and may also be flattened by storage and shipping. Linen and nylon can be broken in quite easily, but both materials tend to tighten on wet days. Although they will be taut the next day, too, they can be quickly broken in again.

One of the most expensive webbings is clock cord. This material reacts slowly to wet weather. Therefore, the stick will be more dependable on both dry and wet days. On the other hand, clock cord requires a longer break-in time. It also takes longer to re-shape after being wet.

A stick pocket should not be so deep that a *whip* will be created. When a pocket is too deep, the ball strikes the top gut strands as it rolls from the stick. This will cause the ball to be aimed downward. A shallow pocket will make it easier to *quick stick*. This means you catch and shoot the ball again in as little time as possible. Also, a shallow pocket will make your passes harder and more accurate.

The depth of the pocket depends upon the player's position. A feeder and a crease attackperson will probably want a shallow pocket. A goalie or a player who dodges often needs a deep pocket. A deep pocket will give more control when catching and cradling. But added depth makes it more difficult to release the ball when throwing.

After playing catch with a new stick, beginners often make another mistake. They may decide to shorten their sticks. A short stick makes it easier for a beginner to pass and catch, but a shorter stick is not as useful in games. No matter what position they hold, all players will have to do some defensive playing. A longer stick will make checks easier at great distances. Also, a long stick will let a player reach for high or wide passes.

Players up to the age of twelve or thirteen should use sticks shorter than high school or college players. Younger people often use sticks that are too long for them. If they are attackpersons, their sticks should be no longer than about forty inches. Midfielders might use sticks about an inch or two longer. Defensepersons would be wise to play with sticks between four and five feet long. Goalkeepers should have sticks about forty to fifty-two inches long.

Remember that once a stick has been shortened, it can never be made longer. Use careful judgment before deciding the length to cut the lacrosse stick.

Once you have the right stick, practice time has come. Just as a basketball player continually shoots baskets, lacrosse players should work to better their basic skills.

Holding the Stick

The problem most new lacrosse players experience is grasping the stick too tightly. In addition, beginners often grip the stick too close to the head. This may feel more comfortable, but the player will lose power when releasing the ball.

Stand with your feet apart. If you are right-handed, grip the butt with your left hand. Your right hand should grip the stick palm up. Your hands should hang down naturally or slightly outside your hips. If left-handed, your left hand is on the stick and your right on the butt. There should be about twelve inches between your hands.

Be sure that your hand covers the butt completely.

Left: This is the correct way to hold the stick if you are right-handed.

Right: The first step in throwing the ball is to bring the stick back so that your upper hand is about even with your shoulder.

If even an inch or two of the stick is showing, an opponent can check your stick and free the ball.

Throwing the Ball

The first skill that a new player should master is throwing the ball. Beginners are often surprised at the similarity between throwing a lacrosse ball and throwing a baseball or football. The stick is merely an added part

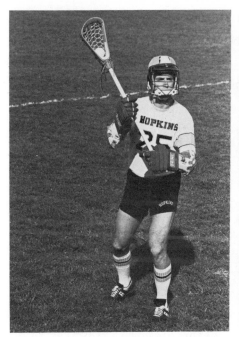

Left: The wrists are snapped and the stick brought forward.

Right: At the end of the throw, the stick is pointing directly at the target.

to your arm. You can throw the ball one-handed or with both hands on the stick. The two-handed throw will have more power.

The stick is brought back so that your upper hand is even with, or just above, your shoulders. The lower hand should be about six to eight inches from your body. The upper hand helps to give accuracy to the throw. This hand also works with the lower one to provide power.

Just before the ball is thrown, the stick is pulled back a bit. Be sure to snap your wrists as you bring the stick forward. Be careful not to use a pull-down movement with the lower hand. Both hands should work together.

Practice throwing the ball while standing still. Aim for accuracy, then accuracy plus power. Next, begin throwing at a slow trot and then a full run. In order to throw the ball while running, you must learn another skill: cradling.

Cradling

This is one of the most difficult, yet most important, techniques to learn. Cradling is a needed skill for catching the ball. Also, a player has to run full speed and keep control of the ball in the stick. The only way to do this is by cradling the ball as you run.

Cradling means rocking the stick back and forth. A beginner usually tends to cradle the ball too fast. Rocking the stick too quickly will cradle the ball right out of the pocket. The stick should be cradled in a smooth motion. The upper hand and the wrist do the cradling. The lower hand merely holds the stick loosely, which allows the stick to turn easily. Be sure not to use only the wrist. The entire upper arm and hand should be doing the work, too.

As you begin to learn how to cradle, watch the pocket. The next step will be to cradle the ball without watching the stick. Once you've developed a feel for cradling, try using the skill at a slow run. Slowly increase

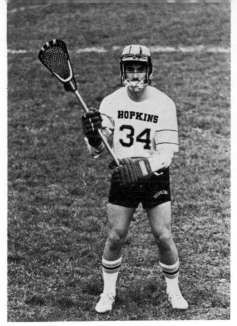

Left: To catch the ball, stand with your feet apart, and make sure the stick pocket is facing the approaching ball.

Right: This player is using a two-hand front cradle as he runs along the field.

the speed. Complete control of the ball while running will not happen quickly. Be patient and keep practicing. Soon you will be able to run at top speed, cradle, and watch the field all at the same time.

Catching

Once you have learned how to cradle, you can begin catching a passed ball. You should stand with your feet about shoulder-width apart, facing the ball squarely. The stick pocket should also face the oncoming ball.

The catch is made by reaching out for the ball. But don't keep your arms locked. Catching a lacrosse ball is like catching a baseball. In baseball, you also reach out

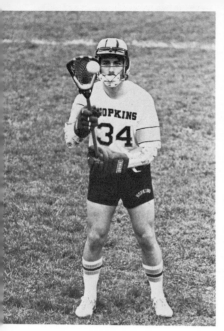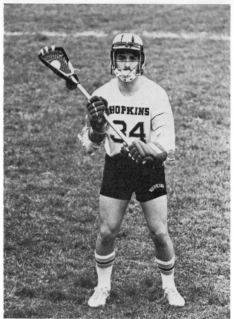

Left: Reach out to catch the ball as you would in baseball.

Right: As the ball enters the pocket, bring your arms back, cradling the stick.

for the ball. When the ball hits your glove, your hand moves backwards to cushion the impact. Otherwise the ball will bounce out of your hand. The same thing will happen if you do not bring the lacrosse stick back toward your body. As the stick comes back, cradle the ball so it will not leave the pocket.

When a ball is thrown directly at your body, all the players except the goalie should sidestep. That way the ball will arrive on your stick side. A goalie should learn to catch without sidestepping. To do this, slide your lower hand upwards. This is one of the few times you should ever move your lower hand.

If a pass is thrown too high, reach far up with the stick or jump to get greater height. You may have to slide your hands down the stick. In this case, there will be a loss of control, but expert cradling will help keep the ball in the pocket.

The most difficult ball to catch is the one thrown to your offside. Don't change your hands on the stick. Swing your body so you face the side from which the ball is coming.

Once any kind of ball is caught, you should turn. Make sure your body is between your stick and the nearest opposing player. Don't turn the wrong way and bring the stick in front of your body because an opponent could check the stick.

Scooping

Being able to scoop up a ground ball is a must for any lacrosse player. During a game, the ball is on the ground a number of times. Controlling the ground balls means controlling the game because you will have many more chances to score.

Beginners often want to scoop a ball one-handed. Do not attempt that. Coaches rarely allow even their best players to execute one-handed scoops.

Success depends upon good body and stick positions. As you approach the ball, bend your knees and upper body. Your back should be almost parallel to the ground. But keep control of your crouching body. Don't fall forward, and don't place any weight on the stick.

The stick should be at a thirty degree angle to the

To scoop a ground ball, crouch and place the stick a few inches in front of the ball.

ground, and it is important that the butt be held to your side. If you fall while holding the stick in front of you, the handle could cause an injury.

The stick head should touch the ground a few inches in front of the ball. Beginners often make the mistake of placing the stick head too close to the ball, with the result that the ball hits the stick or goes completely over the stick head.

As the ball enters the pocket, you should raise the stick. Be careful not to move the stick too fast or too high, thus causing the ball to leave the pocket. When the stick is about a foot off the ground, begin cradling the ball.

You cannot scoop up a ball which lands right at your feet. Kick the ball in the direction you wish to go, and then scoop up the ball.

One type of scooping is called *raking,* but don't try to learn this skill until you have mastered scooping. When raking, your body and stick are in the same position as when you scoop a ball. But you should reach over the ball, bring the stick down to the ground, and draw back so that the ball is pulled toward you. Raise the stick, and then scoop the ball as it rolls in your direction.

Playing With Both Hands

When you begin catching and passing, you will do so on one side of your body. Each person should use the side that feels the most comfortable. But you will want to learn how to hold the stick on the other side, too. Don't rush into this. You may feel awkward when you first try switching sides. Also, you will confuse yourself if you try to learn a new skill with both hands. Master the skills with one hand first. Then try switching the stick.

This talent will prove to be a very helpful one for certain games. A defenseperson will find that he or she can always cover the opposing player's stick. The player will be able to protect the stick and feed quickly. So practicing with both stick positions is well worth the time and effort.

Quick Stick

Another way to improve your skill is to develop a quick stick. This means cutting down on the time between the moment you catch the ball and the time you pass it.

To quick stick, draw back the stick head a split second before the ball hits the pocket. Then, in one motion, catch and shoot the ball, but don't bat it. Quick sticking, however, does not insure accuracy.

A different skill that will give you more control over the ball is the *quick wrist*—a quick cradle with the hand and wrist before shooting the ball.

Quick sticking and quick wristing can be mastered by practicing with a wall. If you stand about five to ten yards from the wall, you will be forced to react more quickly when the ball bounces back to you.

You can practice any of the techniques described in this chapter by yourself. All you need is a wall and a lawn or a playing field. Throwing, cradling, and catching can be done by using a wall to make the ball rebound to you. A lawn or playing field is good for scooping and raking.

Offensive and Defensive Playing

There are other skills a lacrosse player needs to develop. These are the techniques used in offensive and defensive playing. Included are the basics you can learn in order to improve your own playing. Detailed plays usually come from a coach.

Defensive Playing

Every lacrosse player will have to do some defensive playing during a game. Therefore, each team member should know the defensive techniques.

When playing defensively, do not focus your gaze on only one thing. The attacker's hands, stick, and eyes may give you clues to a possible play.

When the attacker has only one hand on a stick, he or she is probably not going to shoot or pass. A defensive player, however, is always alert when the attacker has two hands on the stick. The placement of the stick may tell you from which direction the attacker expects a pass. At other times, the stick may show where the attacker is planning to pass. The attacker's eyes may also give away that fact. Only the best attackers look in one direction and pass in another. Some players' eyes brighten when they spot an open player. This will be a warning that they are about to pass.

Your *footwork* should depend upon the opposing player's footwork. Run so that your hips are even with the opponent's hips. If the person is moving at a slow to half-speed pace, you should use short, choppy steps. If the opposing player picks up speed, you should also.

Basic checks, made with the stick, prevent an attacker from passing or scoring. They also can be helpful in freeing a ball so that your team can take possession of it. The *poke check* is one of the best. To do this, shove the stick through your upper hand, using the lower hand. In a way, this is like using a pool cue. Just before you push your hand, draw the stick back a little, to give your check more power. The check can strike the handle of the other player's stick. Or you can aim for the cuff of the glove holding the butt.

The *slap check* is a short, slapping blow with the stick. Aim for the attacker's lower gloved hand. You can also hit the stick handle just above that hand.

Only the most experienced players should try the *over-the-head check*. The defense player reaches over the other player's head and aims for the throat of the stick. This frees the ball. Some players prefer to do this check with only one hand on the stick. But much control is lost by doing a one-handed check. Control is important

Player 36 will use a poke check to make Player 27 lose the ball. He is aiming for the cuff of the opponent's glove.

Shoving the stick through the upper hand like a pool cue causes the opponent's arms to move, and the ball leaves the pocket.

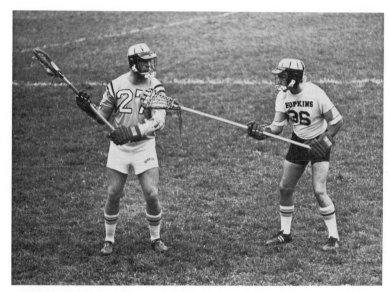

Begin a slap check by aiming your stick in a horizontal position or up to an angle of forty five-degrees. Try to strike the lower gloved hand or the handle of the stick.

Deliver a quick, slapping blow.

This is a one-handed, over-the-head check. Using only one hand, however, means losing control. You might accidentally commit a foul.

because this is a dangerous check. Unintentionally, the player might hook or hold the attackperson and be charged with a foul.

The *wraparound check* is equally dangerous. Again, the problem is controlling the stick. Hold the stick with only the upper hand and straighten your arm. By snapping your wrist, you can wrap your stick around the other player. Check his or her stick. This check is difficult when a right-handed player is playing another right-handed person. The same rule applies when two left-handed individuals are playing each other.

No player is allowed to *hold* another player. But the rules permit holding off a player who has the ball. You may use your closed, gloved hand on the stick handle or you can use your forearm. But your hands must always stay on your stick. Only use holds when the opposing player is charging the goal or is in a good shooting area. Otherwise you will not be able to get support from your teammates.

The *forehand hold* is effective when a right-handed defense is playing a left-handed attacker, or the reverse. Place the heel of your lower hand into the upper arm of the other player. Your stick should be slanted upwards at a forty-five degree angle. By doing this, you will be ready to check the other person's stick.

The *backhand hold* is used when a left-handed defense is playing a left-handed attack or vice versa. The forearm of the upper hand is placed against your opponent's upper arm. Your stick should remain across the front of the opposing player's body. You can then check the opponent's stick when the player attempts to shoot or pass.

When using both the forehand and backhand holds, spread your feet a bit wider than usual. This will give you good support. A defense is allowed to push the attacker with either hand or the forearm. But this has to be done from the front or side; your hand must stay on the stick.

Offensive Playing

Techniques of offensive playing will be needed when your team has possession of the ball. You can either aid a teammate or score yourself. Therefore, all players on a team must know offensive basics.

When two players work together they are often *cutting* and *feeding*. The cutter is an offensive player who gets to a strong position before the goal. The feeder then passes the ball to the cutter. Close teamwork is a must for this quick play. The cutter is usually a midfielder, while the feeder is generally an attackperson. Only one midfielder should cut at a time, otherwise the area in front of the goal will become too crowded. Also, the cutter must wait for the feeder to be in a good spot to pass. If the feeder is too far away, the ball may not reach the cutter.

Once you have decided to cut, try to get your defender in a weak spot. Make the defender think you are going a different direction from the one you plan to go. Hold your stick on the wrong side, and look in that direction, as you are cutting. The defender will think the feed is coming in that direction. By doing this, you will gain a few steps when you break the opposite way. Hold the stick closely to your body as you cut. When you are a few yards from the crease, raise the stick. This will give the feeder a target. Quick sticking or quick wristing will help you score. Your defender's check is going to come fast and powerfully, so get the ball into the air again as quickly as possible.

If you don't receive the ball, there are several things you can do. You can break to the other side of the crease and see if you can get a feed there. Or you can return to the midfield so that another cutter can try the play. Do not stay in the crease area for more than five or six seconds because the playing space will become cluttered with players, and no one will be able to score.

The feeding play works well because most feeds come from an attackperson behind the goal, and the opponents' goalie is in a weak position. He or she is watching the attack and the ball. The goalkeeper often does not have enough time to spin around and stop the cutter's shot.

Being as close to the goal as possible is important for a feeder, since there is less danger of a pass being intercepted. If a feeder keeps the defender moving, the constant motion will help make the pass successful.

The feeder must always be hunting for a cutter. If feeders become too worried about their defender's actions, they miss the teammate cutting in for a pass. Don't give away your play by watching the cutter too much because the defender will guess where you are going to throw the ball, and will probably be able to check the pass.

Vary the strength of your pass. Instead of knocking over a nearby cutter with a powerful throw, try to pass to the cutter's stick side, slightly above the cutter's head. This will make it easier for the cutter to make a quick goal shot.

Being able to *dodge* successfully will enable you to get past your defender and move the ball down the field. Most dodges are made because the opponent has made a mistake—possibly a poor body or stick position. If a dodger causes the mistake, he or she can take advantage of the defender's weakness.

Protecting your stick is the most important thing to do during a dodge. To prevent a check, keep your head even with the stick head and between the stick and your defender. The opponent will not be able to check your stick without hitting your helmet and will be penalized for a foul.

Another kind of dodge is the *face dodge*. If you have the ball and you see that your opponent is going to use a slap check, pull your stick across the front of your body. Actually, the head should be in front of your face.

You can help set up a face dodge by faking a pass. Look at another player and even call his or her name. If your defender raises the stick to block this fake pass, you can use the face dodge.

Perhaps the most commonly used dodge is the slow-moving or fast-moving *roll dodge*. If you have the ball and are moving ahead, a defense player may be waiting for you. The defender will probably try a stick check. Hold your stick as vertical as possible. You can use one hand because this dodge depends on expert footwork. As you move into the roll dodge, swing your lead foot opposite the stick. Pivot and throw your hips into the opponent, but don't strike the other person with too much force because you might bounce off rather than roll on the person. Rolling on the defender's body, will prevent the player from moving the stick. Keep your own stick in front of you, but don't hold it too high because the opposing player might be able to check it. And don't move the stick until you are a few steps away from your opponent because a stick check may be made against you.

The third major dodge is the *bull dodge*, one you might want to use to get to the area in front of the goal. Hold your stick with only your upper hand and keep the stick head even with your own head. Your other hand should be held in front of your body in order to prevent poke or slap checks. Speed is the most important factor in the bull dodge. You must outrun your opponent. Since the offensive player knows when he or she is going to dodge, the defender is often left behind. If your path is slightly curved, you probably will be able to outrun the opposing player.

The player on the right has begun a bull dodge. Holding her stick in front of her, she charges ahead of her opponent.

Practicing defensive and offensive playing will help your lacrosse game. Your expertise in these skills will make you an outstanding player, and your team will have higher scores and more wins.

SIGNALS

Stalling	Tripping	At Face Off Ball In Possession	Brush Off	Illegal Body Check
Offside	From the Rear	Below the Knees	Delay of Game	Pick Off
Time Out	In or On Crease	Pushing	Score	Illegal Procedure
Cross Checking	No Score	Illegal Touching Ball	Slashing	Unnecessary Roughness
Technical Foul	Face Off	Unsportsmanlike Conduct	Out of Bounds Direction of Play	Holding

Many high school lacrosse players now start training at an early age. Since the 1960s, women's lacrosse in the U.S. has experienced a period of growth, although it remains strictly an amateur game.

The Future of Lacrosse

Lacrosse does indeed have a bright future. Each year the number of teams and fans multiplies. People who enjoy lacrosse become devoted to the sport. They go out and round up newcomers because they know that attending a few games is enough to make anyone fall in love with the game. Sports writers and sports casters predict that professional lacrosse will soon be as popular as football, tennis, and soccer.

Eamon McEneaney ranks as one of the outstanding players in collegiate lacrosse history. He is a three-time First Team All-American, and was named "Player of the Year" by the U.S. Intercollegiate Lacrosse Association in 1977.

Both professional and amateur lacrosse have become popular spectator sports.

What is your future in lacrosse? At one time most lacrosse players weren't taught the game until they entered college. But in recent years all that has changed. Little League and high school lacrosse players are now being trained at a much younger age. Professional lacrosse players advise young people to start learning and practicing the game as soon as possible. The beginner should buy a stick and a ball and play catch with a friend.

If your school does not have a lacrosse team, you might ask a teacher to form one. Or perhaps a Little League team could be organized in your town or city.

Once people have watched a lacrosse team in action, they will realize that it is one of the fastest and most challenging competitive sports.